Praise for *What Trammels the Heart*

In Kelly Fordon's courageous, haunting, and formally inventive *What Trammels the Heart*, the illusions are exploded. The catastrophe is implicit and omnipresent. The reader/witness is tortured by an awareness that a very real monster has arrived, is already feasting on us, is making us its own.

Michael Lauchlan, author of *Running Lights*, Cornerstone Press

In *What Trammels the Heart,* Kelly Fordon dissects and confronts, with clarity and courage, the effects of cruelty on the innocent, trusting, or naive. I deeply admire the nuanced way Fordon's exquisite poems thread through emotionally blasted personal stories—her own and others—to create a fabric that portrays myriads of abuse. Here is what Gregory Orr would call poetry as survival. *Finally released,* by the end, *from some grim interior*, Fordon leaves us with poems drenched in light.

Terry Bohnhorst Blackhawk, author of *One Less River*

What Trammels the Heart

KELLY FORDON

Printed in the United States of America

Permissions
Stephen F. Austin State University Press
P.O. Box 13007, SFA Station
Nacogdoches, TX 75962
sfapress@sfasu.edu
936.468.1078

ISBN: 978-1-62288-284-7

First Edition
Production Manager: Kimberly Verhines
Designer: Karina Chacon

What Trammels the Heart

Contents

I

III

I

For my father and Fred

Close Call at OLV 1981

Then there was foursquare,

JP playing dungeons and dragons,

all the girls in a clutch turning

double Dutch. On hot days, we

wandered across MacArthur,

followed the train tracks, slipped

under the fence into the reservoir,

despite the eels. The days were long

and filled with a heavenly light.

We were nine years away from

Tom Chleboski. We still had

Red Rover and the long climb up

onto the roof of the church where

we sang, *I'm on top of the world*,

and lucky we were to believe it.

John Doe

More than half a century ago, a priest
touched John Doe. He was just a boy
in a small village in Italy. A wonder,
hulled, he made it out alive, half man,
half mute. Silent, crippled, steering clear
of interaction, his wife cold in their bed.
An ironworker, he wore a hard hat. Still,
he suffered constant blows. He lost his job,
his wife. A hologram of a man, his children
considered him. In 1988, he made a sign
and traveled down to Mass, paraded up
and down in front of the Holy See, came
back the next day with the same message.
He's been standing on that corner
for three decades.

In My Neighborhood Park—DC

When I lived there, I was often unhappy but
        I had the pillars, the cicadas, the rough feel
of ironwood bark. How the tiny minnows
        glided over the mossy rocks, and I trained
my eye on the forest canopy, longing for
        a lush life. I would not have been
surprised to see a fairy emerging from behind
        a Jack-in-the-Pulpit or a Cheshire cat grinning
down at me from the footbridge. A striking
        bamboo stand had sprouted from a single stalk
planted by a diplomat. While I scouted for rocks
        everyone else was saving the world. They never
entered Battery Kemble Park or rested
        on a fern bed or shared a slice of strawberry cake.
But I had the bluestone walls for climbing and
        in the deep forest, a fort fashioned from
the remnants of an abattoir.

Confessional

I slipped in between the folds and sat in the dark hot box
examining my conscience and waiting for the screen

to slide open and the keeper of the keys to materialize.
His was not the face of a stocking-faced burglar,

or a postman, or the creeper who used to circle my block
in his white van, but it was not the face of God either.

God would not have fingered a clump of pellets while
peppering me with allegations. He would not have said,

Are you sure that's all you've done?

When I was little, I saw a supposed saint, the marquee
attraction in the basement of a famous church.

In her glass coffin, she lay with her hands pointing towards
Heaven, rosary beads coiled around her waxy fingertips.

It was chilly in the temperature-controlled room.
According to the sign, she'd been lying unmolested

for hundreds of years. *Good for her.*
One touch and I turned right to dust.

The Witness

has recurring dreams of tidal waves.
        Waking to a 30-footer crashing through
the bedroom window. The Witness likes the sound
        of the player piano in the living room; for hours
it scrolls through jittery jazz sets. Sometimes,
        The Witness jumps on the bed. For short bursts,
he forgets about the encroaching storm. The Witness
        loves the groaning stairs and the sound of
family members flipping in the kitchen. The Witness
        has survived another night. If he had a superpower,
he would take on the witch doctor who roams
        the streets scattering magic pellets. The Witness
loves the saying: To each his own. In class,
        The Witness sings "Joy to the World" and John
conducts with his hands. There are no other performers
        in this pit. Eighth grade brings sorrow, the lone robin
on the tree branch outside the classroom window in February.
        Miss Fleming in her flat black shoes. Norman Watkins
in his wheelchair, his ever-present nasal drip, his
        silly jokes, the way he grabs hold of The Witness's
wrist to share his latest nonsense rhyme. The Witness
        still loves the feel of marble, he loves the incense,
the God who materializes genie-like when the priest
        pours first the water and then the wine into his goblet.
The Witness's job is to replace the empty cruets. Years later
        his job is to squceze his eyes shut until he can hear
the dodge ball thudding against Eleanor, or Elizabeth
        screaming *out!* The way the woods glowed with lime green
leaves in the early morning light and the house was
        sometimes suffused with the smell of strawberry cake.

Hummingbird

The nectar has grown milky
and clotted. Fodder for the ants.
Still you flit around me
waiting for sweet release.
Oh, fly away! Don't look to me
for sustenance. I don't even know
how to feed myself.

My Mother

My mother was a mirror. Perhaps,

you've heard this one before.

The mirror with special effects—

not convex, concave, plane, fun

house. No. Just one way. Slant

so the light hit the coating and tipped

into darkness. I could see into

the room but not a way out.

Light receded first, followed

closely by hope. Perhaps another

daughter could have breached it

or walked in and shattered it.

Instead, I just waited for a glint

or even a crack.

First Dog

Grownups had better things to do.
You got used to it, there was
the dog. The dog smelled terrible,
but you could not have loved her more.
You learned to think of yourself
in hypotheticals, in the second person,
but the dog was Shannon, she had
a name. She liked to swim, she shed
too much. In the woods she'd approach
anyone. Sometimes you walked her into
shadowy places where the babysitters
couldn't find you. You learned early on
to avoid them. Perpetually petrified,
you hid under the bed, in the closet.
Shannon wasn't much of a guard dog,
but she was affectionate. Unlike the
babysitters who snarled, bared their
teeth, wandered through the house,
long-limbed monsters dragging
their coarse and knotty knuckles.
Shannon hid under the bed,
you with a blanket in the closet.
After they found you, you moved
to the bathtub, then to the attic.
So she didn't technically save you.
Maybe no one could have, but you
had a witness. It was something.

Battery Kemble Park

Soldiers stationed
at the union army defensive site
adjacent to my childhood home
pillaged residents' pantries
and we were no different—
barefoot, charging here and there,
taking what we needed
and mawing on it.

The Maddox tributary
tittered like a girl anticipating
her first slow dance,
the rocks made jagged headrests,
the sun rippled her fingers
through the pine boughs,
sh, sh, sh.
We'd secured the perimeter
or so we thought.

One day, a bearded man
bared himself by the bamboo.
An older girl piloted me
up to the highest parapet.
It could have been any year.
We could have been anybody.
We could have been detached
or in search of reinforcements.
The enemy came close.

What Hair?

after Rapunzel

You cut it, blunt, boyish, called it hair of a mouse,
or a tumbleweed, a sleeping skag, a humming
string, a ragged thatch, a detached planet.

Nothing here but scattered leaves, jagged branches,
no wall, no tower, just a stand of wretched revelations,
a tattered screen revealing zilch. Mother,

when you asked me what I wanted, I requested
blue barrettes—fortune favors the bold. Unsettling
sounds emanated from your mouth. Were they helpful

words or terrible musicians? I made myself heavy, so
I didn't float off, the chattering coming from the trees
was me. The bird became a boy who flew across the room

and landed at my feet. I remember the sugar, how you
hid it on the high shelf. I longed for a tiny elf, one to
slap me on the back with a *way to go*, or a hand

reaching down from heaven, a shoestring rhapsody,
the light from the sky hitting my stone dome, to feel
like this moment was not a smash, that you wouldn't

just explode, or kick the dog, that when I entered
the room, your seraphs might lay the red carpet. Where
are my dancing shoes and the rat-a-tat-tat? Where are you,

Mother, your rosary beads a-clackin'? In a story I
once loved, I lived with you in that tower. In a story
I once loved, we entered another portal.

In a story I once loved, the road rose up to meet us.

This Year

The year when a little piece chipped off,
a broken shovel, black ice on the road.

Without hope, I raged at the gibbering fish,
posting, posting, posting, nothing clicked,

like fingerless gloves, cold where it counts,
pin cushioned faces. Fiend, I called those

who brought us low, but is the fiend in me?
The world on fire, but not the universal one.

So much misinterpretation, minds like vessels,
overflowing. Fox in the den, fox on the loose.

Some injected it, and some kept buying it,
both the meal and the candlestick maker.

A man touched me while I was sleeping.
Then scolded me for remaining awake.

On the Train I Thought of Chagall

I saw a long line of cars.
I saw a big white house.
The ground was mottled
and abraded like
the back of a buffalo.
I saw a chicken coop,
a muddy ditch,
the padded cell
of the sky.
I saw a hunting blind,
a telephone poll,
ratcheting arms,
coal silos, sand silos,
yards like ratty bath
towels, abandoned
sandboxes.
No green man.
No benevolent cow.
No villagers whistling and
hoisting sickles.
No multi-colored houses.
No woman waltzing
on the wind, Chagall.
It was the morning after,
the tough rows to hoe,
the scrub brush of babies
and midnight feedings,
Kansas before the witch's
stockings and the wizard's
charade. No tree of life,
just my chalky fingers
on the windowpane,
just my face pressed
against the glass.

The Witness Plays Dodgeball

On an April day dense with wounded weather
Bill got hit on the full; down he went. The Witness

emerged from the office two hours later. No
memory of the door or the knock. The Witness

missed the dive and the final elimination.
He missed first and second lunch. The Witness

turned into the wimp on the line who drops
or punts, who knows no bounds. The Witness,

the kid no one wants on his side, the one who
would rather kip than compete. The Witness

is a mark now. He never dodges the blow.
He's always first man out. The Witness

had *not a scratch on you* that day. Forever
more, he'll bear the mark. The Witness

on a continuous loop through the drop
and the shock and the moment The Witness

woke up, covered in grime, his friends calling
his name: *Bill, Bill, Bill.*

II

Medjugorje

In 1988, my mother took me to Medjugorje in what was then Yugoslavia, where some shepherd children had spotted the Virgin Mary. According to the shepherd children, Mary appeared like clockwork every night at 5:00 PM. Sometimes, the sun spun wildly in the sky. On the plane to Medjugorje, I met a beautiful, red-haired man from Boston. I wanted to be sane again, and he wanted to be straight.

We prayed and prayed.

Mistake

In 19█, I attended ████ in ██████████ and made the bad Catholic girl decision to go up to a bedroom with a boy I liked. I was sixteen. The boy and I sat on a bed and kissed. When I told him I didn't want to go any farther, he said, *Well then, we can just pretend* and he held me down by the wrists and ground away on top of me for what felt like an eternity. We were both fully clothed. During the whole sordid sequence, no matter how hard I tried to extract myself, I could not move, and that sensation of his hands on my wrists has ██████.

That was ██████ *horrible,* I thought afterward, but my mother had warned me that when boys are "excited" they often lose control, so I blamed myself. Only a slut would have gone upstairs with him. Only a fool, according to my mother, would assume that a boy wants something other than sex. I did not like what he had done, but because I assumed he was a normal boy and this was normal behavior, I went out with him again.

In the back seat of a car on our second so-called date, he held me down and yanked my underwear off.

We've waited long enough, he said, then he ████████.

I said stop

over and over and over and over and over over and over and over and over and over over and over and over and over and over over and over and over and over and over over and over and over and over and over over and over and over and over and over not because I realized I was being ██████—I did not. I said stop because it hurt.

He did not stop.

I told no one.

I didn't even consider telling anyone because

I had asked for it.

Shame on You, Said

the rapist.

We both know
it was consensual.

I went up to the room.
I liked you.
And then,

Stop spreading
lies about me.

No. No. No.
No. No. No.
No. No. No.

My parents don't believe you,
they're behind me.

No one blames me
more than me.

Shame on you.

If I continue
to feel bad,

You followed me like a dog.

I can always

It was consensual.
If you don't stop lying,
I'll press charges.

take myself out
of the equation.

What are you trying to achieve?

If it happened
and no one saw,

Don't you know, nothing
good will come of this?

it must not
have happened.

Or maybe

Nobody cares.

The Witness Went Back

Same two steps up to the altar,
same candles, same long wicks,
the space behind the altar,
the many grooves in the oak seats,
the way the light filtered in blue,
the rooms in the back
where everyone lined up.
The robes felt like sheets
sliding over a corpse, the rope
had a ball on the end, the people
closed their eyes, singing about
loss and redemption,
services interminable,
the only place to find God
was in the blank stares,
the way the head
sometimes separates
from the body,
how if you look carefully
you will find that people
are just floating heads
transported by a trunk
and appendages that soil easily.
But the head can leave the body;
it's been done:
people with headphones,
people staring into space,
people with their heads down
praying, chanting,
missing everything—
where do they go?
Where did The Witness go?

Excuses Excuses

If nothing else, words make fine moats.
No ice cream truck, just a white hat
and strong fingers, a ream of paper cones.
Grounds wound round like yarn. The ladies
in their wide-brimmed hats waving *hello.*
An old man pinging pennies against
the mending wall. So you planted a tree,
but who hears the luckless among us?
Dirty towels, rusty syringes, a shredded
mattress; please don't call it a shrine
by the roadside. Some say God passed
through on the night train, but if so,
he must have turned a blind eye.

Monster in my Mirror

It's a big world and I wish I had a little rhinestone suitcase. Then I could carry you around like a miniature poodle. Of course, you are much smaller than that. You could hide behind two books on my shelf, you could fox trot with the dust bunny under the couch, quiver in anticipation of the broom. There! Over there! You could dart underneath the tea set. You could nestle into that score in the wood. Once, long ago when you lived in the crib, I believe I remember you larger. I saw you shaking the slats. Escaping must have been scary! That may be when you shrank a la Alice, crawled underneath the wall-to-wall carpet. Set up camp there. Later, in the hospital, your size saved you, scurrying as you did up the IV pole and into your own vein. You made sure the infusion took. I will put you in an eggshell, in a locket, in a coin purse, under my tongue. Never mind what they say about you. You are not alone. Look in the woodpile, on the evergreen leaf, in the finch feeder, there are hundreds riding in the paramecium parade. Stick to the glue on the envelope and I will lick you. Someone will post you. You can pretend that wherever you are, there you aren't.

Going Through Security

An old man placed his case on the table,
unpacked his sorrow and all its long
tangled cords. A woman in a wheelchair
kicked off her cowboy boots and
her companion placed them gently in the bin.
Another dumped the dregs of her
purse out as if inured to shame.
The teenager's hold fit together:
computer, cables, cell, all vital.
When my turn came, I peered down
at my pack, which lay on its side
like a body part, bent elbow or knee.
I know exactly what you need,
the woman in the wheelchair said
to me, before she was hoisted to her feet.
Hold your hands up, said the guard.

Stone Enclosure — A Ghazal

My maiden name is a noble one, crusaders,
warriors, politicians, the first part = stone.

Last night before the howling wind and waves,
the lake might have been a giant stone.

An anchorite is a recluse walled into the side
of a church in an enclosure made of stone.

I have always had an affinity for them—
sealed in, pent up, safe behind stone.

With lake levels rising, the bluff demolished,
people pay handsome sums for armored stone.

What is contained—what has been pressed—
strangled, trampled, muted into stone?

When I chafed against the clergy and her own
constraints, my mother's face turned to stone.

During the pandemic, we shelter in homes,
prefab, wood, and all manner of stone.

But our enemy is wily—capable of filtering
even through fissures between the stones.

No wall will keep the lake from taking a home,
waves wear down even seven-ton stones.

The anchorites died within their cells,
The Lord couldn't save them—nor the stone.

What trammels the heart—tamps it
into grit and pulverized stone?

I miss the people who loved this lake,
who now reside beneath stone.

This moniker so well-fortified—safe-
guarded, as impermeable as stone.

Yes, Stanton feels the allure. I hope
she never spurns the world for stone.

In September 2018

My classmates from [redacted] Preparatory School spent a lot of time discussing the Brett Kavanaugh confirmation hearings. Of the roughly twenty classmates I talked to out of 100, four admitted they had also been assaulted during high school.

*Kate: Assaulted at my house during a party by a boy who I would have said seemed completely harmless. I was shocked to learn that this happened in my own home while I was there. She never told her parents.

*Rosie: Assaulted in a bar. Never told her parents.

*Ann Marie: Assaulted by a boy at a party. Fled the house and barely escaped. Lost a shoe. Terrified he was going to rape her. Never told her parents.

*Me: Assaulted at a party and then in a car. Same perp. Never told my parents.

Four out of twenty (20% of our entire class) in an informal poll. There had to be others, but how many? Some of us might have been spared if we had shared our stories back then.

But we didn't talk.

After the Confirmation

And this will be rebroadcast.

Before it happened I was damaged.

True.

Cast in stone, and the impending dread.

Doom and premonitions on every billboard.

Everyone saying *perhaps* *perhaps not.*

He said/she said, and on and on and back

and forth. I came unglued.

All those who "knew" him *just knew.*

My memory? Only two people

in the room. Now, the whole audience peering

through the squint.

Own your behavior, the jury said, as He

got off.

Perhaps you have seen this performance before?

Questioned the veracity of a lived experience?

Relegated your own perceptions to the backseat?

Shame flooding in through every orifice.

Mind filled with sludge.

The Alp

Akin to the incubus but with magic hat.
The cap of concealment. Shapeshifter.
Small, white butterfly. If you see one
coming, lay a broomstick under a pillow,
hang iron horseshoes from the bedpost,
place your shoes against the bed
with the toes pointing toward the door.
If you awake to find an alp, ask him
to return in the morning for coffee.
He will beg not to be turned away. Plug
up any holes, specifically key holes.
An alp can only leave the way he came.
A light kept on during the night will
ward off an alp. A sentry may also be
employed to wait for the attack.
The alp may be driven away if caught
by someone not under the alp's influence.
And isn't that always the case?

Pose

I found the old footage before the move.
My mother behind the camera coaxing me.
Pose for me, she commanded, the red eye resolute.
I wanted the car keys; she had to be placated.

She had to be placated; I shrank from her gaze.
Such a shock to hear my sugar voice, soft as gauze,
sheer as Saran, slim as a shroud. Susurrations
from a sickbed, Whispers—

I had been trained to whimper.
Like the dog underneath the table.
Like the dog cowering.
Like the seagull outside, soundless.

Like the seagull outside, the wind a forever foe.
She pointed out my flaws so I could capture them.

Dear Mother,

Once mother. Once upon a time. How the king

swooped down and caught you in his net.

Neck.

As in snapped. As in mine. Oh, mother, such a wild

ride, such ferocity, such

conviction.

A bus filled with pilgrims singing as the convoy

sails over the cliff. Those who seek the promised land

strewn with mines.

Oh, mother. Once upon a time, mother. I owe you

something, but what?

And what of me here in this white room

with the ash scattered and the rocker stationed

at the window. It's winter.

Even the trees are cowering.

All day long, I listen with my ear against the earth

for something to germinate and lift, for

the ground to part, for the shoots to emerge,

for you to materialize on a shiny leaf

as if your exodus was just

a temporary matter.

Hands

Before I placed my bones down on the table,
lined them up from frontal bone to foot,

before the gentle knock and the dim lights,
I paced the streets, raging at the maple tree,

red tongues bright and ululating, the beech
dangling scythes of sunlight. Back and forth,

forth and back as the branches snickered, and
the crossing guard flicked his big stick, and I

recalled that on this quiet street, the lunch lady
succumbed first. A moment like a fin darting up

and then back under dark water. The masseuse
knew none of this, though she knew better than

to talk. Those of us who remain slap against
this shore like so much bilge, sewage

decomposing in the mouth, neighbors,
once kind, planting signs of ruination.

Grant me peace, I said to her hands. Let me
remember what it feels like to be touched.

The Anchorite's Dream

1.
I see a wavering mind,
a flag blowing in a courtyard.
I see the tunic of the Lord
like a bright light   all

around me

2.
A room attached to a church,
a small slit in the wall.
People pass victuals,
and sometimes

minutes

3.
I know the apple
tree at the end of the lane,
and the town crier.
What he says is

pressing

4.
Whatever I choose,
God has foreseen it.
But who would choose
this?

close your little window

5.
The hand remains open.
The days   the same
as the nights   when
you are   enclosed.

the alliance

6.
I am waiting for Him.
When I can't sleep,
I press   my eye
into the ground

the bricking in

7.
Bats bed down
in the   spires,
little   white crosses
line   the lawn.

it's all the same

8.
God has a sapphire eye.
Can you hear the passersby?
Alone on this barren earth,
coat the color of sky,

your breath on my neck

9.
He is my father, my mother,
my much loved bride.
Everyone sings
even the devil,

my wounded lover

10.
The shadow
moves around.
It's behind you.
It's behind me.

the mother knows

11.
A dancing maiden, grows
older, grows colder.
The swan spreads her
wings across the sky.

All Shall Be Well.

12.
My kind mother,
My gracious mother,
My dearest mother,
take pity on me.

deliver me

13.
from this life,
from this pain
and suffering,
into the bliss of

heaven

14.
The fiend is at my throat
his face long and thin,
his hair red as rust.
The fullness
of joy

is the leave-taking

Libertas non est sine pretio.

They Don't Come Back

I heard a siren and wondered who's next?
        The lunchlady killed crossing the street.
This somnambulant town filled with peril.
        One friend moved away and promptly died.
I feel the urge to rhyme to stave off sadness,
        They don't come back. They don't come back.
My father in his gray suit and my other love
        who drank himself to death. When people leave
They don't come back. They don't come back.
        I'm doing it again; I wish this was a jingle.
Something to crochet and hang upon the wall.
        A pithy epithet, a couplet, words to soothe,
herbal tea. At home on the couch, day bleeds in
        to night, it's time for prayer or not. Either way…

In the Portland Japanese Garden

Somebody you loathe
is shattering to pieces,
and somebody you love too,

so why not behold
the mountain on the horizon,
the white peaks grazing

the sky, and the visitors
lining the benches
in this Japanese garden,

perfume rising from all
the bruised petals
blanketing the ground.

After Sappho

Speaking of desire, what shall I call
the drumming of my heart? Sweet,
racing violets. Dream dialogue
with blossoms. Artemis holding
a goblet filled with the finest sand.
The honored child, the winged lady,
the sweet-smelling grass, I've never
seen them. The road has loosened
my skin like a cloak, and all the gods
in my head lament this poverty
of song, trapped as they are
in their separate dungeons. When
I feed them, they sometimes say:
You shall know love, but not until
your tongue sheds its bitter robe.

Lament for My Religion

The cruets,

    the candles we lit with long wicks,

the hymns, the ones who sang off-key

    including my father, the ritual of early

mornings, the donuts served after Mass,

    the Parish, the ballast, the camaraderie,

the conviction our lives were divine,

    a person who would die for ME,

a small cubicle where sins were forgiven,

    grace like a hot toddy, a fur muff.

But not so much the shame of incessant

    sin, the punishment, and remorse,

the judgment brought down on the kids.

    The horror

on betrayal, the automatic tick,

    the automatic tick, the lack of sex,

the lack of enjoyment, the lack of self-

    respect, self-regard, the inability

to look other people in the eye,

    the shame, the shame, *the shame.*

This is Not a Poem

It's the house
and the sinkhole.
It's the deck
and the sand underneath.
It's the moment
the mountain gives way.
It's the lake
and the storm on the horizon.
The sunset
and the clouds obscuring it.
The robe
and what he wore underneath.
The arms he lifted
and the place they landed.
God's outstretched hand
and the ravine in between.
It's a small dog safe in her crate
whose vocal cords were cut
by an old woman in a trailer.
It's the beatings the dog endured
and the day I rescued her.
The years she cowered
under the couch
and the day she surfaced.
No, this isn't a poem,
it's the only sound she can make.
It's not pretty, and she knows it.
But she still wants to live,
and you can't stop her.
You are not the worst thing.
You are not even close.

III

The Believers

after Ambrose Bierce's The Devil's Dictionary

Grey sky and lime green trees,
Jesus floating
near the telephone poll.
Land of the fanatic.

People plodding.
Cars zooming past.
On the corner, the zealot
with his pamphlet.

In Medjugorje,
Mary keeps her standing appointment
with the hillside visionary.

Sometimes, God throws plates
or plants a small blue stone
in a blind man's hand.

Once, I met a woman who thought Source
had instructed her
to pardon the devil.

Any shepherd,
horse whisperer,
cowhand
or ne'er-do-well
can be a prophet.

Shall we shaketh our arrows
or just bow as the elect
approach the exit?

We are right   about everything—
candidates and mandates and
the final standings.

The days are getting longer,
the days are getting shorter,
yet another sign from above.

Conviction and self-righteousness
and nothing on Sundays
save the fool's fuel.

The ten commandments
etched in stone
and set aflame.

Later, we'll chuck the plates.

Mourning

A snowflake landing on a warm pane.
A fly agitating between glass and screen.

People gliding by, stencils on parade.
Silence as indictment, benediction, curse.

A voice sounding out over an empty field,
over this town, this alarm clock life.

When we were young, we held hands
and peeked over The Cliffs of Moher.

I will never go again.

State of Denial

I am not apologizing.
For many years, I was a glad
hander, I waved in your parade.
But the nights were long and
filled with gleaming teeth.
I told   you
what you   wanted
to hear. And then,
I told you
what you wanted
to hear.
At night, under the mattress
I kept a list of truths,   little people
with torches, tucked away,
beneath the hospital corners.

Fanatic

after the Netherlandish Proverbs by Pieter Brueghel the Elder

We have all been here before, tarts on the roof,
scissors hanging, my mother could tie the devil

to her pillow with a hangman's knot,
and you bet her mother dropped down armed

to the teeth. What can smoke
do to iron though? A pillar biter, my mother,

leading people around by the nose.
Though she's not alone, so many followers

pissing against the moon. Who knows why
geese go barefoot? Why, my mother, of course,

gnawing on the rock, and me, looking
through my hands. I am not the warden. She

answers to the keeper of the keys, the one who ties
the flaxen beard on Christ.

Hollow Words

The safe zone. The spot under

my chair the dog has staked out,

We ignore the cluck of disapproval

from the other diners when I feed her.

How disgusting she appears, more

rodent than canine. She's past her prime,

but I like her more than almost anyone,

my hand reaching down to her wet mouth

and returning slick with microbes.

What to do but lick them off as

the other partygoers discuss who

does their hair and where they had

their last *thing* done, who cares

which one? Nobody here speaks

the truth—folks paying lip service;

intent on decapod decimation.

Sitting at this outdoor table, clavicles

like soup tureens, eye sockets

as purple as greater yams, I might

as well be on the bottom of the sea

in Kamchatka, sludge floating up

and spilling out along the shore.

Everyone blithely swimming along.

The Witness Hates Everyone

And who could fault her?
She hates men, the way they made her feel
like a bauble tossed, the way they mis-
handled her. There were robes, they were white
like Cinderella's gown, they were soft and light,
and you cinched your robe with a cord,
you cinched it tight; the priest showed you
how to do it, he put his hands around your waist.
Many nights in the bathtub counting tiles,
one, two, three, who is going to save me?
There was a long wick to light the candles
and in the tabernacle, the body of Christ.
The body, the body, the body. The many uses
and degradations of the body. Here we go again.
The Witness must say *the body* 313 times,
she must turn the lights on and off 313 times,
she must say his name, his name, *his name.*

Dear Believer,

Do diamonds rain down on Jupiter and Saturn?
Will a frog in the pitcher stave off sour milk?
Is Jesus the ladder to heaven; do angels hoist
buckets *of what?* Maybe they water the grass?
This morning such a surreal green, and then
the day shed her yellow coat. A tom ambled past
my plinth with his winterkill. Who needs a witness
and her bitter tears? My mother
believed my sins would be forgiven, but
the priest had other plans.
Most of the perpetrators keep rising, regardless,
clutching the rungs, squashing the innocent.
It must be cold on that ladder—bone-chilling.
The gatekeeper fumbling, humanity like lint balls
clinging to his robe, all the zealots and jeremiads
scrabbling up the folds. I can hear the faithful
booing as I push these words out like slugs.

Hand me another apple.

Dear Believer,

She left me for the Lord.

He is king after all. Let no man

come before him, or, in this case,

woman. She's a believer,

not a mosquito skirting a bug zapper—

she believes marriage lasts forever

unless you dissolve it

in a basin full of molten

gold. Some so rich,

they've liquified four—

some not so lucky. Take

the woman whose husband

forgot to drop her annulment

envelope on the counter before

he skipped town. *The nerve.*

And now my son

who is gay—

and mighty fine, I might add—

is going to hell, according to *the believer.*

Excuse me while I LMAO.

Is there any room left in hell?

Because I know a few priests.

I hate to say it, but if the believer is right,

then God is an asshole.

Right now, I'm dictating this rant,

and this dictation device doesn't

want to call him an *******

but what other word works? Not

the good word. There's no

bliss bubbling up in this gold chalice,

no Rose of Sharon blooming

in my personal desert. Bring on the crown

of thorns. I've read every page

of the Victims' Testimony—and watched

survivors helicoptered in

for a weekend of camaraderie, before returning

to their own respective nightmares. On the first

night, a scream sounded out that I'll take

to my grave. All a long way of saying

the believer left me for hard

wheat bread and men of questionable *****.

She believes the Lord—given myriad choices—

prefers their company. See why I have

such a bad impression of him? Still, I'll admit it,

I'm sad. Who wouldn't appreciate

a pinch of grace, a smidge

of benevolence? I can't find it anywhere. Perhaps

my children are the keepers of the keys,

or the neighbors peeking out from behind the blind.

Once upon a time, the believer

stood by me, once upon a time

she held me in her arms. Once upon a time,

I issued forth from between her legs.

It was hot, it was messy, it was a human birth.

Oh, mother, mother, *mother.*

Riding the Bus Downtown

I went back to get my umbrella.

Love is a never-ending cup.

Everybody is on foot or underfoot.

Oh, how the fireflies light up the night.

Easy for me to say see you tomorrow.

So many sideways glances.

Valentines for the displaced.

If I could, I would shut your eyes.

My father loved Glenn Miller.

A fact no one but me now knows.

Friend, you cannot get off here.

In the Hospital

the gilded elevators
the gilded elevators are   beautiful

the muffled chatter
the muffled chatter
in the waiting room is   beautiful

the receptionist
the receptionist's
wandering eye   beautiful

the pages
the pages
in their black pants
and crisp white shirts   beautiful

the blonde woman's
wedge cut   beautiful

the bright blue
plastic bags   beautiful

the swirly design
on the soothing blue carpet   beautiful

the nurse and her sad,
ragged hair   beautiful

the whooshing
of the operating room door beautiful

the old man shuffling past
with his walker beautiful

the carmine scrubs
the plastic shoes beautiful

the sky, though gray,
is still there beautiful

isn't the wispy white hair
of the elderly man beautiful

aren't his hands
with the toothpick bones beautiful

every wall
every mark
every scuff

beautiful
beautiful
beautiful

Nobody Touches Me Now

On my dorm room wall
I had a poster of a tabby cat
And one time, *was I high?*

He touched me with love *you heard that right*

it was pretty spectacular
better than the other one

insane
ok
maybe he didn't

but I felt it

in that sad room

one time
a poster of a cat
looked down on me
with love *not the other way*

so I still
believe in God

that's all I have *nobody touches me now.*

Funeral Day

An alarm sounded—
flood warning—over
spill. My throat like
a culvert, swamped,
the path impassable.
When we were young, I loved
everyone. Now I see
only failure, mostly mine.
We lost touch.
This morning,
coffee flowed down
my shirt. And then
why not?
Implosion therapy.
Stones, debris, fallen
limbs, another coffee
flowing out
all over the floor.
A song came on the radio:
Send me an angel
Send me an angel
Send me an angel
right now.
The funeral was held
in a church, so I had
no choice.
I am not worthy
to have you under
my roof,
everyone chanted,

before consuming
the cracker.
Then my mouth closed
and my chin
jackhammered
my chest.
Kneeling,
kneeling,
kneeling,
so many people with
their hands pointed
toward the ceiling.
The priest
sensed my cock-
eye, though I kept
my head down and
never screamed once.
My friend was dead.
He described her
like you might describe
your plumber, *Nice man,*
meant well, always came
when called.
No mention of
the beach, the
blue, the blue
boutonnière, the day
bowing down
before us,
sand in our toes.

Dear Believer,

I hung your silence on
a hook in my bathroom
Under my robe—soggy,
mildewed.

I dragged your silence
around like an X ray apron,
a gurney, a dead dog.

I planted your silence
in the yard to mock
the perennials,
to choke the grass.

I stirred your silence
into my tea like arsenic,
like bleach, like sand.

Your silence sat beside me
in the front seat—so
vulnerable, obstinate,
so imposing.

Your silence in the theater—
riveting, damning.

How I wrestled with the devilfish of your silence.
How it wriggled its way into my bed, clammy and sad.
How the great lake outside the window rose to meet it.
And the sky unzipped to receive it.

How I stood you for all those years despite it.

The Good Word

**After The Four Apostles, by Albrecht Dürer*

in the beginning
the word and the garden and the apple

all of that *good*

the apple tasted *good*

was it good or not good

because Adam looks unhappy
and Eve a little drunk

was the knowledge
good or not good

god or not god

as in
Adam has never found me attractive *not good*

as in the world is a strange
and silent place with no people in it

as in the world outside this walled garden
might be filled with chocolate croissants

but the crucifixion was *not good*
and the book under lock and key *not good*

who would want to lord that over us

in the beginning the father was right
in the middle

he was *a good god*

though stern and aging and weak
and mumbling over the beads

his son suffered
head hanging
barbs
around the crown

all so
unequivocally *not good*

so why leave it all
to the keeper of the keys

stingy with the word

perhaps he realized

one day we'd wake up and grasp it

god *we're good*

The Good Dream

When she gets in the car, she's groggy.
She keeps asking how I managed

to wake her, as if there was some trick
to it, and we laugh about the spectacle

of the hospital gown, the dangling ties,
where do they go and what good

are they anyway? We commiserate
about the cold, which was pervasive,

and the nurses who surely self-medicate.
We both decide the doctor looked as if

he'd just backed into a hot stove.
It was all over so quickly. *She's going*

to be OK, the doctor said, and then
seemed insistent—the only moment

that caused pause. As if I'd ever argue
with good news. *She's alive!* The sky is blue.

Outside, spring's bounty. We drive to 7/11
for Slurpee's. We have trampoline feet.

Luxembourg Gardens April 2022

Like Hammershøi's wife finally released from

some grim interior, I sat in my pale green chair,

watching the old men play Pétanque, as

children screamed and chased a football.

It was late afternoon, war was raging, somewhere

nearby, a careless college girl expectorated into

her mask. Twenty years to the day since my father

died. Like all good dreams he had seemed so real

and now he was like the little boy's sailboat circling

the Medici fountain, the more I reached for him,

the farther he drifted. Across the gravel path,

clover carpeted the lawn. Soon I would have

to leave this paradise where people once raced

velocipedes and twirled their parasols. I pictured

Berthe descending from her dais, bending one

stiff knee then the other—I've been frozen too long.

Hall, Montana: Easter Weekend

The family left me alone here at this ranch
on the night before Easter, so I'm holding
vigil for my old life, the one with the Peeps
and the Creeps, the swarms of sinners
and saints, not nearly as sublime
as the view right now, the mountains
snow-capped, the river like a mad rush
of silver fairies racing toward
who knows where? The dog, Molly,
as black as if she's just emerged
from the lake of fire, her eyes
like some amber liquid that would
do me in in a hot minute. I'm
listening to Andrea Bocelli, and I
don't miss any of it, not the wafer
nor the wine, not all the time I wasted
on shame, the nun with the half-finger,
how she wagged it in my face,
my mother yanking me out from
under the table where I was kissing
my little friend, Alexandra. We'd just
seen *Billy Jack* and we didn't get it.
Until we did.

My mother spent this whole weekend
in church, praying for forgiveness.
She's her mother's daughter—
not the source, just the moon reflecting
off the barn sash window. I'd like
to hold her up like a spray of forsythia,

sprinkle her into the creek, watch her
spin like a helicopter on whitewater.
There's only sky out here, no one
but me and the wind. I can't carry
this anymore. Like Molly with her
deer leg, maybe I'll bury my bitterness
in the middle of the prairie.

Maybe it will transmogrify.
Maybe it will feed me.

Acknowledgments

The Antigonish Review, "Luxembourg Garden, Pose, They Don't Come Back, Dear Believer, Let's Pretend Jesus Meant It, and Nothing Stops Us," 2024.

Mobius: The Journal of Social Change, "The Good Dream," 2024.

NonBinary Review Issue #34: Lies for Children, "Dear Believer," November 2023.

Anti-Heroin Chic, "They Don't Come Back," August 2023.

Panoplyzine, "What Hair?" issue 23, 2023.

Thimble, "First Dog," spring 2023.

Bear River Review, "In My Neighborhood Park: DC," 2022.

Ruminate, "Dear Mother," 2022.

On the Seawall, "The Lunch Lady," August 2022.

Sepia Journal, "Hands" and "Our Lady of Victory 1981," 2022.

Frontier Poetry, "Easter, Hall, Montana" November 5, 2021.

Rogue Agent, "Sappho," May 1, 2021.

Women's Studies Quarterly, "The Witness Plays Dodgeball" and "Gaslighting" *WSQ Together,* Fall/Winter 2019.

Isthmus, "The Good Word," summer 2019.

One Jacar Press, "This is Not a Poem," 2019. Pushcart nomination.

Poetry Center Chapbook Exchange, "The Witness" Chapbook one of five chosen for the chapbook exchange in January 2017. https://poetrychapbooks.omeka.net/

Some of these poems were published in "The Witness" Chapbook published by Kattywompus Press, 2016. Winner of the Eric Hoffer Award for the Chapbook and shortlisted for the Grand Prize.

2012, Finalist in the Anam Cara poetry award for *On the Train I Thought of Chagall.*

Notes:

Close Call at OLV 1981
Tom Chleboski:
https://www.washingtonpost.com/archive/local/1991/05/24/dc-priest-gets-22-years-for-molesting-va-boy-13/ee46ad67-8b56-469b-9b35-daf97f006237/

John Doe
Inspired by many activists like John Wojnowski:
https://en.wikipedia.org/wiki/John_Wojnowski

The Witness
Poems are derived from suvivor stories. See the Survivor's Network of those Abused by Priests:
www.snapnetwork.org for more information.

Medjugorje
A village in Bosnia and Herzegovina where the Virgin Mary has allegedly appeared since 1981.

Mistake
I am a contemporary of Christine Blasey Ford and also grew up in DC. My sexual assault was eerily similar to her testimony.

Shame on You, Said
A poem born out of several recent rape stories. These assaults took place within the last ten years. In other words, this is still happening.

In September 2018
All names are pseudonyms, and the stories are deliberately vague to prevent identification.

The Alp
Inspired by a painting at the Detroit Institute of Art by Henry Fuseli called "The Nightmare":
https://dia.org/collection/nightmare-45573
https://phoebedarqueling.com/2020/11/20/fairy-tale-friday-the-alp-in-german-folklore/

Dear Mother
The Catholic Church allows and, in some cases, endorses discrimination against the LGBTQ+ community. Ultimately, who deserves the blame for a belief system—the parent or the institution?

The Anchorite's Dream
The translation I used for "Libertas non est sine pretio" is:
"Liberty is a thing beyond all price." (Corpus Iuris Civilis)

The Believers
Incorporates some words from "The Devil's Dictionary" by Ambrose Bierce and attempts to match his flippant tone—a tone one adopts as a last ditch effort to stave off despair, in my experience.

The Good Word
Refers to "The Four Apostles," by Albrecht Dürer. Dürer created

the painting as a warning against fanaticism:
https://en.wikipedia.org/wiki/The_Four_Apostles

Luxembourg Gardens April 2022
The Danish painter Vilhelm Hammershøi's wife often appears in his interiors, and like many of his figures, is usually depicted from behind "as if absorbed in something that the viewer cannot share."
https://www.journals.uchicago.edu/doi/10.1086/684354

Cover Art:

"Untitled" by Kimberly Santini. Santini is a Michigan based painter creating expressive interpretations of her life experiences. She loves inserting duality into her work—what appears to be one thing can often be read as something else as well. She also tucks little painted treasures into her compositions similar to the Hidden Pictures page from Highlights Magazine, which she loved as a child. She has an active social media presence, paints daily and teaches in person and online - you can find links to all of that at www.KimberlySantini.com

Many thanks to the fellow writers who reviewed these pages and to my friends and family.

Gratitude beyond measure to survivors everywhere for your bravery and your voice. Sometimes, it doesn't feel like it, but your testimony makes a difference.

It matters.

Kelly Fordon's latest short story collection, *I Have the Answer* (Wayne State University Press, 2020), was chosen as a Midwest Book Award Finalist and an Eric Hoffer Finalist. Her 2016 Michigan Notable Book, *Garden for the Blind* (WSUP), was a Michigan Notable Book, an INDIEFAB Finalist, a Midwest Book Award Finalist, an Eric Hoffer Finalist, and an IPPY Awards Bronze Medalist. Her first full-length poetry collection, *Goodbye Toothless House* (Kattywompous Press, 2019), was an Eyelands International Prize Finalist and an Eric Hoffer Finalist. It was later adapted into a play by Robin Martin and published in *The Kenyon Review Online.* She is the author of three award-winning poetry chapbooks and has received a Best of the Net Award and Pushcart Prize nominations in three different genres. She teaches at Springfed Arts in Detroit and online, where she runs a fiction pocast called "Let's Deconstruct a Story." http://www.kellyfordon.com

www.ingramcontent.com/pod-product-compliance
Lightning Source LLC
Jackson TN
JSHW020244060625
85686JS00010B/42

* 9 7 8 1 6 2 2 8 8 2 8 4 7 *